# Beginner RIDING

### Written by Jay Swallow
### Illustrated by Joan Thompson

©1990 HENDERSON PUBLISHING PLC

# ABOUT PONIES

## Ages Ago
Prehistoric horse, known as Eohippus, lived on earth between 50 and 60 million years ago. His size was more like a fox than a horse, suited to the forest and swamp. He had toes instead of hooves. As the climate changed over the ages, his shape and stature changed too. Today, we have Equus Callab - the modern horse, or pony.

## Conformation
The various 'points' of a pony, and the overall picture they present when pieced together, determine his conformation. Some points are obvious, like the head, legs and tail. Others need to be learned.

## Measuring Height
A pony's height is measured from the *wither* to the ground. He can be measured in hands, inches, metres and centimetres. There are four inches to a hand, so that a 12 hands 2 inch pony is 50 inches high. The same pony is 128 cm. or 1.28 metres. A pony doesn't grow into a horse. He is 14 hands 2in. and under, although a hunter pony is 15 hands and under.

2  RIDING

## Colours

The very first ponies were presumed 'muddy' coloured. Today their colours include; brown, bay (a lighter brown), chestnut (chocolate to ginger and golden brown), black, grey (white is known as grey), piebald (black and white patched), skewbald (brown and white), roan (an even mixture of white and dark coloured hairs), cream, dun, palomino and spotted.

## Markings

These are the white patches often found on the face and legs. They include; Star (on the forehead), Blaze (a wide strip from forehead to muzzle), and Snip (a tiny patch on the muzzle). Stockings are white legs from below the knee or hock to the hoof and Socks are from the fetlock to the hoof.

**Long in the tooth**
A pony's age can be assessed by studying the length, grooves and wearing surface of his teeth. Young ponies, like children, lose and replace their milk teeth.

**A question of sex**
A pony stallion is a male capable of fathering (siring) foals.
A gelding is a male incapable of siring foals.
A mare is a mature female.
A colt is a young male.
A filly is a young female.

**A world of ponies**
There are over sixty breeds of pony in the world today. There are also countless types, part-breds, crossbreds and ponies of mixed breeding. A 'type' signifies a colour, such as albino or palomino, or a purpose, as in the polo pony or the hunter pony.

Purebreds are of a single breed. Part-breds and crossbreds have two or more breeds to their make-up. A great number of ponies have an infusion of Arabian blood in them to improve their agility, speed and endurance.

4 RIDING

## British ponies

England, Scotland, Wales and Ireland have, between them, nine different breeds of native pony. These are termed Mountain and Moorland ponies, and are famed worldwide for their hardiness and stamina and their ability to withstand inclement weather conditions on the minimum of grazing.

These pure breeds are the Welsh, Highland, Fell, Dales, New Forest, Connemara, Dartmoor, Shetland - the smallest of all, and the Exmoor, which is the oldest breed of all. British ponies have been exported all over the world.

## Scandinavian ponies

Sweden has the oldest Scandinavian pony, namely the Gotland, but the Norwegian Fjord pony, the mount of the Vikings, is the better known.

He is dun coloured (biscuit), with a black 'eel' stripe running the length of his back and rump and through the centre of his upright mane. He is very strong, sturdy and useful for harness, riding and as a pack pony.

**RIDING** 5

## N. & S. American, Canadian and Mexican ponies

Imported British ponies abound in America, but the country has established its own two breeds by crossing the British Shetland with a high-stepping Hackney to obtain the 11.2 hands American Shetland for riding and driving, and the pony of the Americas by crossing the Shetland again with the spotted Appaloosa for a larger 13.2 hands.

South America has the Criollo, of Spanish Andalucian and Arab descent, and also the tiny 7 hands Falabella.

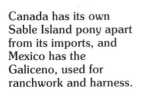

Canada has its own Sable Island pony apart from its imports, and Mexico has the Galiceno, used for ranchwork and harness.

## Australian ponies

These ponies are derived from a mixture of Welsh Mountain and Shetland crossed with Arab, Thoroughbred and Timor (Indonesian) blood. Again there are many other British native ponies to be found.

## Universal ponies

Ponies from the Continent, Asia, South Africa, India and Russia have existed and been worked hard, for centuries. Many are derived from very old breeds, like the Mongolian of Asia, and the Camargue of Southern France, known as the 'white horses of the sea'.

## Appearance

Ponies are large or small, smooth or rough-coated, narrow or thick set, sure-footed or speedy according to the climate and terrain of their origin and the uses for which man has purpose-bred their descendants.

# USE OF PONIES

**Master and servant**
For centuries ponies have been used as the servant of man. Initially they were a source of food and clothing for man, the hunter. The wandering nomad tribes soon learned that the wild ponies of the region could be trained for transport as pack ponies and riding.

**Domestication**
As time advanced and horses were excelling in chariot racing, jousting, warfare, as mounts for kings and desert Bedouins, in the bullring and for ceremony, the more menial tasks fell to the pony. They were the carriers of arms and supplies. They worked in the field, on the unmade road and tracks and on ranches as sheep and cow ponies. They fetched and carried food and implements to and from outlandish and uncivilised regions. Red Indians and Romanies were zealous pony owners, revering especially the spotted and 'painted' ones.

**Coloured ponies**
Piebalds and Skewbalds are often termed 'coloured'. Spotted ponies came originally from Spain to America in the 16th century as the mount of the Spanish Conquistador. The Red Indians of the Palouse Valley of North America loved them and bred from those that were left behind. Hence a spotted pony became known as a Palouse, and today is an Appaloosa.

RIDING 7

## Mechanisation

Before the railroads and the combustion engine modernised the industrial countries of the world, the pony was indispensable. Perpetually in harness, he delivered bread, groceries, milk, butchery and farm goods in a domestic capacity. He delivered post and other communication items. The Pony Express of America is a tribute to his work power. He carried and pulled commercial goods - coal and tin in the mines, threshed corn and took it to the barn, pulled logs from the forest, took peat to the hearth and carried the shot deer home over mountainous country.

## Entertainment

The gypsies raced their ponies along the roads in competitions to see whose pony could trot the fastest. Travelling circuses used ponies for performing tricks, the riders standing up on their backs and swinging under their bellies. Children went fox-hunting on ponies, and adults used them in polo games and put them in harness classes in shows to see who owned the highest stepper.

## Today

Today the pony is still the cheapest form of labour and transport in the undeveloped, third world countries where they are almost worked to death. Only in Western civilisation has the pony at last come into its own as a loved and well cared-for child's pony.

# LEISURE AND SPORTS

- **Just riding**
  Many ponies are kept and loved by children purely for riding at leisure, hacking and exploring unspoiled country, either in company or alone. Pony Trekking, in its organised form, is becoming a very popular activity, especially for those children who do not own ponies.

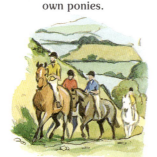

- **Competitive riding**
  Other young riders are more competitively minded, and their ponies have to fulfil, in many cases, a great number of sporting requirements. Once a child has learned to ride, and the pony is well trained and obedient, the versatility of the combination is endless.

**Clubs and shows**
Ponies and children get together by joining various local and national pony and riding clubs. The British Horse Society Pony Club was founded as long ago as 1929 for the purpose of encouraging young people to ride and enjoy ridden sport. There are now over 1000 branches in Great Britain and most English speaking countries. Horse shows in the English speaking countries and on the Continent cater for Show ponies, Mountain and Moorland ponies and Western Riding, all for junior riders.

**Jumping**
Among the sporting activities open to child riders, perhaps show and cross country jumping are the most ambitious. Starting at local show and 'nursery' level, through to national and even international level in show jumping and eventing, these activities are quite possible for the young rider from 7 to 17 years old. Eventing incorporates Dressage as well as show and cross country jumping in its three phases and requires the performance of a memorised test of set movements, in a marked arena, to prove the pony's obedience and suppleness and the rider's ability.

**Gymkhana and mounted games**
Not all children, or ponies, enjoy jumping. Ridden races, like bending, sack race and apple bobbing provide competitive fun for fast, handy ponies and capable, agile riders.

**Team games and mixed events**
Children in the Pony Club can now compete in Branch Polo and Polocrosse matches. There are also Penthalon and Tetrathelon events incorporating shooting, running and swimming as well as riding.

# TRAINING A PONY

### Why training?
Ponies must be trained or 'broken in' before they can work. Training starts when a foal, through handling, halter breaking (teaching to lead), and generally teaching control in all situations. Most ponies start their real training, for riding or harness, at 3 years.

Early training
Ponies start their lessons by learning the words of command on a lead. In the English speaking countries, these words are usually 'walk on' and 'whoa'. Riding 'tack' (saddle and bridle) or driving harness is then introduced. Lungeing (circling the trainer on a long lead) follows, during which the pony learns to 'trot on' or 'canter'. Driving with two long-reins with the trainer on foot, using the same words of command teaches the pony to obey the signals from the reins.

Unfortunately, in many undeveloped or third world countries, ponies pull or carry heavy loads far earlier.

### Early training
Ponies start their lessons by learning the words of command on a lead. In the English speaking countries, these words are usually 'walk on' and 'whoa'. Riding 'tack' (saddle and bridle) or driving

### Backing
A pony is 'backed' when he learns to accept and carry a rider for the first time. The procedure should be calm, quiet and in an enclosed space, one person holding the pony and another 'legging up' the rider. When the pony shows no fear or irritation he can be lead forward, answering to the words of command from the rider.

**RIDING 11**

## Further training

Once a pony is happy to carry a rider and obey his commands through voice, hands and legs, he can go independent of a leader or the lunge. Primarily he will find it very difficult to balance himself and his rider in anything other than straight lines. Turning and circling in both directions and at all paces on smooth, flat ground are all part of his training and schooling curriculum. This work requires a sensitive and experienced lightweight rider, for he must never be hurried or bullied.

## Specialised training

Jumping, gymkhana, cross-country, dressage and polo are subjects for 'A' level training, and can only be undertaken when the pony is thoroughly versed in 'O' level groundwork. He must be at least $4^{1}/_{2}$ or 5 years and then under the eye of an equivalent human specialist.

## Experience

Throughout his training the pony must become accustomed to the farrier for trimming and shoeing. He must become oblivious to road traffic and all the alarming objects he may meet on a ride. He must also learn to load into a trailer or horsebox.

# SADDLERY

### Tackle this!
Saddlery is the term used for saddles, bridles and all other equipment designed for the control of the ridden pony and the comfort of the rider. Harness is more aptly used for the equipment required for driving the pony. Both are referred to as 'tack'.

### First things first
The earliest of the old world riders, and the Red Indians of the new world, controlled their ponies with leather thongs around their noses. They sat on cloths made from pony skin. A difficult animal may have had a thong drawn through the mouth. Saddles with girths and stirrups, and bridles with metal bits were a later variation designed for control and comfort.

### Mediaeval to modern
The saddles used for jousting and ancient warfare were clumsy in comparison with today's streamline models. Ladies rode sidesaddle and required a *pommel* over which to drape their resting leg. Likewise ranch riders required one to attach the roped steer. Soldiers required gadgets to accommodate swords or guns.

Today we have as many different designs of saddle as purposes for their use. There are different patterns for jumping, dressage, racing show classes and all-purpose riding, although western 'cowboy' saddles have changed little. All saddles should clear the pony's spine, as pressure can injure his back.

RIDING 13

## Bits and bridles

Although there are dozens of *bit* designs today, each providing a different method of control, the most acceptable for the child's pony is the *snaffle*. This is jointed or straight, has rings at each end and provides for one rein in each hand for the rider.

Today it is generally made of stainless steel, though rubber or vulcanite are also used. When attached to the bridle, the whole piece of equipment is termed a snaffle bridle.

## The saddle

Saddles are made of leather, felt or man-made material. The *stirrups* and stirrup leathers are fixed to iron bars at the top of each side (skirt). The girth keeps the saddle in place, being attached to straps under the side flaps. Learn the different parts for discussion on placement and use of tack.

## Cleaning

Saddle soap will keep leatherwork supple. Dismantle, clean and oil your tack regularly, looking out for any dangerous wear on it. The bridle, stirrup and girth should be cleaned at least weekly.

# RIDING CLOTHES

### Safety hats
The essential item of clothing for the rider is an approved hard hat. This can be purchased from any good Tack Shop or Equestrian Clothier. It must have a safety chin-strap and conform to British Safety Standards. Other countries may not be so strict but under British Pony Club, Jumping and Eventing rules, riders cannot compete without a safety helmet.

### Jodhpurs, jeans and so forth
Jodhpurs are ideal leg protectors because they do not 'ride up', causing rubbing and pinching by the saddle and stirrup leathers. Likewise, breeches worn with high boots. Jeans, workmanlike trousers and chaps will suffice for leisure riding. Never wear flimsy or fashion pants or shorts. Skirts are out, except for side-saddle riding.

### Boots, shoes and other footwear
Jodhpur and high riding boots are ideal with jodhpurs, breeches or trousers. Lace-up shoes with a low heel and smooth sole are next best. Buckles become caught in the stirrup irons. Flat, heel-less shoes or trainers slip through them. Wellington boots or ridged sole footwear become dangerously lodged.

## Weatherproof warmers

All are suitable for lessons or leisure-riding. Shirts with long sleeves look better than T shirts and act as protection against scratching and fly bites. Do not dress flamboyantly but be conservative and complement your pony.

## Show and competition wear

There is a 'uniform' in keeping with various riding activities. Show turnout requires a riding jacket in black, navy or tweed; a collar and tie or stock; jodhpurs, boots and gloves. Event riders wear coloured sweaters or shirts, and bright silks over hard skull caps. Polo players wear a different style of hat. Western riders wear Stetsons, fancy waistcoats and chaps. Before entering any type of competition, become familiar with the turnout required.

Whatever the occasion, competition and show clothes should be scrupulously clean, well fitting and in good order. Long hair should be tied, coiled or netted for tidiness. Earrings are taboo.

## A word in your ear

Relations wishing to see you ride in a cross-country event for the first time should be advised to come in suitable clothes. Flat country shoes or boots, trousers or roomy skirts, anoraks or other country-wear for warmth if it is cold or wet, will be much more 'in keeping' than high heels, a tight skirt and a fancy hat.

# LESSONS

- Expert tuition early in the rider's career is essential. Riding school lessons, at a licensed establishment approved by the British Horse Society or the Association of British Riding Schools are possible in most counties in Great Britain.
- Class lessons are taken at all levels, by a qualified instructor, on safe ponies. Private lessons are also available.

**Where to begin?**
Here are some methods for finding a suitable riding school:

- In Britain, the Yellow Pages of the telephone directory - or its equivalent on the Continent or USA.
- The equestrian press - large establishments advertise in horse and pony magazines available from the newsagents.
- Local 'tack' shops have a good knowledge of local schools in the region.
- Both the local farrier and the veterinary surgeon probably service, and could advise on, an approved school.

Word of mouth - maybe a friend or acquaintance knows of a school in the area.

The local County Council and the Tourist Board have lists of licensed riding centres. If you live in Great Britain, you can also write for details to The British Horse Society, National Equestrian Centre, Stoneleigh, Kenilworth, Warwickshire CV8 2LY for a list of approved schools in your area.

RIDING 17

**Private lessons**
Mobile instructors are becoming more popular, but generally the rider supplies the mount. A few instructors maintain one or two ponies for the beginner.

**Holiday courses**
Many large Riding Centres offer intensive courses at all levels during holiday time, for one or two week's duration. Some centres, especially in tourist countryside, offer live-in riding holidays where pupils learn to look after ponies as well as ride them. Hacking and entertainment are part of the holiday course. (Look in the equestrian press or contact the Tourist Board.)

**Pony Club**
The British Horse Society Pony Club has holiday rallies for members where instruction is given at different levels of riding. Members require their own or a hired pony. For membership contact: The British Horse Society, National Equestrian Centre, Stoneleigh, Kenilworth, Warwickshire CV8 2LY.

**Disabled riders**
Contact Riding for the Disabled Association, Avenue R, National Agricultural Centre, Stoneleigh, Kenilworth, Warwickshire CV8 2LY.

# GET SET TO GO

### Leading
Look at the picture carefully and you will see how to lead a pony. Notice the following points: The leader is on the left (near) side of the pony. She is beside him, not in front. She has two hands on the uncoiled rope. She is looking ahead - never stare at a pony; he hates it. When in the correct position the leader says, 'walk on' and puts forward pressure on the lead with the hand closest to the pony's head. To stop, she will say 'whoa' and pull back with the same hand.

### Mounting
Ensure the pony's girths are tight. Stand on the near side of the pony facing the tail. Hold both reins with even pressure in the left hand. Rest hand and reins on the pommel of the saddle. With the right hand hold the stirrup iron ready for the left foot. When in position, place the right hand on the waist of the saddle. Move around to face the saddle. Put your weight on the left foot in the stirrup. Hop up and swing the right leg clear over the pony's back. Settle gently in the saddle and place the right foot in the stirrup. Pick up reins in both hands.

### No digging
Throughout the mounting procedure, try to avoid digging the left toe into the pony's side.

RIDING 19

## Position of rider

Sit in the centre of the saddle with a straight, but not stiff back. Keep your head up and your hands low. Your legs should be close to the pony's sides, and the ball of the foot in the stirrup. Imagine a line drawn straight down through your ear, shoulder, hip and heel, and you will see that the leg drops just behind the girth. The stirrup leathers are approximately the right length if the irons knock against the ankle bone when the leg is hanging free.

## Holding the reins

Assuming the pony is wearing a snaffle bridle, you will have one rein coming from each bit ring to each hand. The rein runs along the pony's neck and enters the knuckle side of the hand between the third and little finger. It then runs along the inside of the three fingers going towards the thumb where it leaves the hand and falls over the index finger. It is then held gently in place by the thumb. The hands and reins are held with the thumbs uppermost, with the finger nails of each facing each other. There should be a light contact, at all times, between the hands, reins and pony's mouth. Keep the wrist supple.

# PRACTICE MAKES PERFECT

**Signals and aids**
The signals through which the rider tells his pony to walk forward, trot, canter, turn left or right and halt are termed 'the aids'. These are given by voice, hands, legs and seat.

**To walk forward**
Squeeze the pony's sides with your legs and say, 'walk on'. If he is slow to respond, nudge him gently with your heels, increasing pressure of both until response is obtained. Keep the toes up.

**To trot**
Apply the same aids, saying, 'trot on', tilting the body forward slightly when response is obvious. Then, either go with the movement, with a relaxed body and seat close to the saddle (sitting trot) or, rise in the stirrups, lifting the seat from the saddle as the pony takes alternate steps, returning to sitting position with every other stride (rising trot). Maintaining a continual up and down sequence with the pony strides is not easy at first for the novice. It will take practise but, like riding a bicycle, once learned is never forgotten.

**To canter**
Sit close into the saddle and apply the forward movement aids as for walk and trot, saying 'canter'. Sit 'into' the canter, relaxing the back and moving gently from the hips with each stride.

**Leading leg at canter**
As the pony canters you will notice one shoulder moving further forward and with greater thrust, than the other, causing a longer stride. This is his leading leg and is normally on the inside when the pony is cantering a circle.

**To slow down and halt**
At whatever pace you are riding, sit down in the saddle and exert the necessary pressure on both reins until the pony is as slow or as still as you require him.

**To turn left and right at all paces**
Put pressure on the same rein as you wish to turn and squeeze with the opposite leg. Keep the hands together and low.

**Jumping**
This will come much later, and only after considerable ability is gained by groundwork lessons. Basically the pony is kept firmly in line to the jump by hand and leg, and encouraged by more leg pressure as the jump is approached. On take-off the rider tilts the body forward and allows the hands to move forward up the pony's neck as he stretches it forward. The pony's mouth should never be interfered with by the rider losing balance and hanging on to the reins while jumping. This could well happen if you fail to lean forward and go with the movement. It is termed 'getting left behind'.

# PROGRESSIVE RIDING

**More haste - less speed**
Riding cannot be taught in a few lessons, or from a book. It takes months of practise to get through the early stages, and years to become experienced. Do not expect to rise to the trot immediately, or to jump before you can canter properly on either leg.

Even the best riders go to 'clinics' or to other professionals for a 'brush up'. Bad habits can be easily picked up without supervision and, if left, are hard to eradicate.

**The nerve of it**
Some riders are not as bold as others and need time to gain confidence. This is not a fault - in fact the careful riders are considerably safer than the arrogant. Do not say you can ride if you still feel insecure at any pace. Stay happy until you are ready to progress from one stage to another. Remember - *pride comes before a fall*. Also, an unhappy, nervous rider trying to keep up with his or her friends will miss out on the joy of riding and will often end up with a fretful, unhappy pony, too.

## Consideration

Ponies, like people, respond to praise and encouragement. A pat on the neck after something achieved, and a 'good boy' or 'clever girl' is appreciated. A firm hand with a pony who is disobedient is necessary and any admonishment for 'bolshy' behaviour is in place at the time, by a sharp tap of the whip and a growl.

Beating up a pony, hitting it over the head, shouting and abusing is **NEVER** in order, and a sure sign of the ignorant, inexperienced rider.

## Determination

It is admirable to want to master each stage within a series of lessons. However, if you practise without supervision between lessons, consider the pony's feelings. Endless practise, going around and around the same ring, school or field, for your benefit, will eventually bore the pony to tears and may well turn him sour and obstinate. Likewise, jumping a pony continually over the same jump will make him dislike the whole exercise and he will probably end up refusing to jump at all.

A little practise, for a short time, with any new exercise, giving praise when due, will bring much more pleasing results.

# OWNING A PONY

**Pony mania**

Once you have been bitten by the pony bug, you will long to have a pony of your own. Wonderful. The more children who can love and look after ponies, the better. Let's do some hard thinking on the subject ...

**Look before you leap**

It is so simple to go to a riding school, or to a friend, and ride a pony that someone else has produced - that is managed, fed, watered, groomed and often, saddled up. But just look around. The pony has a field, a stable or field shelter, food, hay, grooming equipment, tack, regular visits from the farrier (blacksmith), and is treated regularly for worms, dentistry, vaccination and any accidents, by a vet. All these things are necessary and require money, not to mention the cost of the pony and his insurance, which these days is costly. For example, in England, a very ordinary pony costs from £500 plus, and a good competitive pony is well over double, and can reach £10,000.

## Experience

There is a tremendous amount to be learned about looking after ponies - apart from being able to handle and ride them properly. How good a rider are you? Better to find out from your teacher before a new pony shows you up! Have you read up everything you can about pony management? Have you any experience in looking after ponies, perhaps those at the Riding School or that of your friend? If you have little to go on, is there a really experienced adult in the family or your circle of friends, who could steer you through the responsibility of pony-owning?

## Time

Looking after a pony well requires time. During the school holidays you will have plenty of time, and will probably spend all and every day with your pony - except if your family take you away for a fortnight to some distant holiday resort. Who will look after the pony then? And what about school? An outdoor, grass-fed pony will need looking at every day. In summer this is fine if you are not at boarding school. In winter he will need food and hay, and perhaps the ice breaking on his water. A stabled pony will need bringing in during the winter, his stable mucked out, and regular feeding. If you are at day school it will be dark when you come home from school in December, and icy cold in the frost and snow of February. Are you prepared for this? Or is there someone in the family who is - on a regular basis?

# MORE ABOUT PONY OWNING

**Let's get organised**
Supposing we make a list of everything required before you go any further with your dreams, even plans, of owning a pony. To do this you must first decide whether you wish a) to keep your pony at livery, b) at grass, or c) stabled.

**At livery**
This means that someone else supplies all the facilities and looks after the pony for you, for which you pay a weekly or monthly fee.

**At grass**
Mountain and Moorland ponies can live outdoors, at grass, at home, summer or winter, with adequate grazing and food in winter and some form of shelter.

**Stabled**
A competition-type pony of more refined breeding will require stabling, with daily exercise, either ridden or at liberty. If you cannot attend to him full time, someone else must act as groom.

## The choice
Each category (a, b or c) will require: The pony. His tack. Grooming equipment. Veterinary charges. Insurance. Farriery.

**Extras: Class A:** Livery fees. Often, Veterinary and Farriery come within the account. Livery varies according to season and type of pony.

**Extras: Class B:** Grazing. Shelter or stable. Food, hay and their storage. Fencing and paddock maintenance. Available winter help.

**Extras: Class C:** Stabling and stable equipment. Rugs. Means of daily exercise and management. Hay, straw and food storage. Manure space. Transport to competitions. Stable, yard and paddock maintenance.

## Facilities
If you can share the grazing, stabling or shelter with a friend, the cost of keeping a pony near your home will be greatly reduced. You must of course offer to share expenses.

A field or paddock must be safely fenced. Thick hedges or post and rails are safest and best. Barbed wire is dangerous. Outdoor ponies appreciate a field shelter for shade and relief from flies in summer, but it is not vital if there are high hedges or trees in the field. A single pony requires an acre of grazing. Stabling the indoor pony is very expensive. Quotes from builders or stable and shelter manufacturers are required, and often planning permission is needed before stabling can be built. Don't forget that a pony requires a constant supply of fresh, clean water.

**Finally ...**
Show the last few pages to your parents!

**28 RIDING**

# BUYING A PONY

**The search begins**
Do you now know exactly what size and type of pony you require? Are all accommodation arrangements in order? Then we'll begin.

**Spreading the word**
Let everyone of interest know that you are looking for a pony. That means your Riding School, the local Tack Shop (who will often put a notice up in the shop), the local vet and farrier, your pony-minded friends, the District Commissioner of the Pony Club (or secretary). All these people may know of an outgrown pony, with a good reputation, that may be on the market. Do not pretend to anybody that you are a more capable rider than you really are.

**Advertisements**
Scour the local newspapers. Usually there is a 'Horse and Pony' column. Do not consider any pony under the age of seven, as he will not have the experience to further your abilities. Do not answer an advert that does not fulfil what you have in mind. This is a waste of time to both parties. A 'first' pony is for a beginner. A second is for the more experienced. Know your own standard.

**Understand the jargon**
A pony used 'to all P.C. activities' means he is known to the Pony Club of that area. Check him out. He is a good choice if his reputation fits. No vices means he is well mannered, does not rear, shy, buck, windsuck, crib-bite, kick or bite you, and is easy to shoe, catch and load. Check all this out before visiting. Ask his price if this is not advertised.

**Placing an advert**
Supposing if, after a couple of months, you have not found anything, try placing your own advertisement. Having studied so many adverts, write one in similar style, but saying exactly what you require. An extra long advert may cost more, but may also save considerable petrol and time. Remember, good ponies are hard to find. Young, 'green' (inexperienced) and unsound ponies, and those of doubtful reputation are more common.

**Look hard**
If a pony sounds right for you, you must make an appointment to see and ride him. Always take an experienced adult with you to watch you ride the pony, help you test it out and assess its manners. Look at its conformation and seek out any glaring faults or unsoundness that you may miss and a veterinary surgeon would charge for. There are many questions to be asked, apart from catching, shoeing, boxing, safety in traffic, and behaviour in company. Has the pony ever had laminitis? Does it 'hot up', argue, or kick other ponies? Most important, what is its present diet?

**Riding a new pony**
It will take a little while to get used to riding a strange pony, but if after ten minutes or so you find him too keen, too sluggish, too wilful or too stubborn, say so. Ask if there is anyone else to show him off before you even get on him, so you can see how he goes at his best. If you want a pony for hacking out only, ask if the owner will accompany you for a short ride outside his home ground. If you want a jumping pony, ask to see his rosettes and list of successes and put him over some jumps. If you do not like him at all, do not waste your time or the owner's. He may be just the right pony for someone else.

### Trials

If you come across a pony that you really like, and you feel suits you, most owners will allow any trial 'on the premises'. This means you may be allowed to ride the pony two or three times, under the owner's supervision, to really test him out. However, you must really be interested in the pony to ask for this concession.

A trial away from the pony's home is a different matter. You may be lucky and obtain a week's trial, but few owners like the idea. You could wreck a pony, or another sale, in a week. If you do have a pony for a short time, he must be insured and have extra safe and adequate facilities.

### Veterinary examination

Never buy a pony without having it 'vetted'. A vet will test him for wind, sight and soundness and may well pick up something you or your experienced helper may miss. You will know that he is the stated age and is healthy and sound by having him vetted before a cheque is passed.

### Be honest

If you are not interested in a pony, say so at the time. The 'I'll let you know' brigade are a waste of everyone's time, because they rarely do! Don't be one of them.

# FEEDING

**Food for thought**
Among the things that ponies eat are: grass, hay, cereals (oats, bran, maize, etc.), pony mixes and nuts (which are mixed cereals), well soaked sugar beet pulp or pulp nuts, apples, carrots and vitamin and mineral additives. The pony owner must learn to feed according to the season, the pony's type, and the amount of work/exercise he is given. If you have a new pony, follow his previous diet until you are used to him. A sudden change of diet can upset his digestion and behaviour.

**Mountain and Moorland ponies**
This type of pony will probably need only grass in the summer months when he is doing little or no work. In fact, even his grass may have to be rationed if he becomes over-fat and inclined to laminitis. If he is worked hard, then pony nuts or pony mix will keep up his energy. These two foods, obtainable from a food merchant, are the cleanest, most easily stored and simplest method of feeding. There are directions for diet on the bags, or in leaflets from the merchant. In winter daily hay will supplement the lack of goodness in the grass, and feed may also be necessary, especially if the pony is working in the holidays.

32  RIDING

### The half and half pony

In during the night and out during the day. In winter, this type of pony will need bringing in to a feed and haynet at night, and another small feed before turning out, or riding out before turning out, in the morning. This can either be hand mixed from the variety of foods suggested, or ready mixed food or cubes. In summer, vary the diet according to the amount of work and grass the pony is having.

### The stabled pony

Stabled ponies require 2-3 small feeds per day and hay morning and night. These ponies must be well exercised daily or they will become over-fresh and may develop bad habits and stable vices from boredom.

### Read, read, read

Read all you can about pony diets. The leading food manufacturers have leaflets and diets galore regarding their products, and articles in books and pony magazines offer endless advice. Take it, always remembering to feed according to work and exercise.

# EXERCISE

**Work and hacking**
Working a pony means schooling him. It is giving him mental and physical exercise in a restricted area, while teaching him obedience and suppleness in answer to the rider's signals or aids. He can also be worked over jumps, ie. schooling over coloured poles or cross country fences. Work also involves getting the pony fit for some sporting activity, like hunter trials or Pony Club events for which he will need to be muscled up and prepared to canter long distances.

**Schooling**
Given too much school work, the pony becomes bored and sour. Alternate schooling with hacking and relaxed fun riding.

**Hacking**
Hacking is literally going out for a ride at a relaxed pace and in a free and easy way, with or without other riders. If the pony is to become fit, long trots and steady cantering for longer distances will be required.

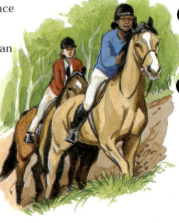

**Boredom**
Ponies become very bored if they remain in the same field all their lives, especially if they live on their own. They need to mix and be ridden with other ponies. Variety is very important, both in environment and in the form of exercise. Someone else's schooling ground, jumps or riding country makes an interesting change.

## Practice and over-practice

It is tempting to over-practice a pony at something the rider wishes him to learn. A pony needs practice if he is to excel in his rider's chosen activity, but little and often is the general rule. Never go on with the same exercise, be it schooling, jumping or dressage, until the pony is fed-up. It will only turn him sour and teach him to search for ways of avoiding the commands given. Improvement will only come while the pony is interested in his job. Refusal to move, rearing, refusing to jump, pulling and avoiding the bit are all caused through work-boredom.

## Bad habits

If bad habits are caused through inexperienced schooling, STOP before too much damage is done. It takes an experienced rider to school and improve a pony single-handed. Advice is always necessary, even in the top flight riders of a chosen activity. A person on the ground can see the pony's outline and way of going far better than the rider on top. If possible, school under experienced tuition, or at least have a month's 'check up' on progress with a capable tutor. In this way faults and evasions can be dealt with before they take hold.

## Bits

It is wrong to consider using a more severe bit when pony does not obey the bit he is using. Often a 'curb' will aggravate a pony into worse behaviour. Seek advice before changing.

# GROOMING

**Catching the pony**
If a pony lives outside, he must be caught and groomed before he is ridden. Take a headcollar and rope lead, or a hemp halter into the field. Take also some sliced carrot, apple, a piece of bread or a small amount of food. If you are feeding from your hand, make sure it is held completely flat so the pony does not mistake a finger or thumb for the tit-bit. Otherwise use a food scoop. Walk quietly up to the pony, talking to him and showing him what you have for him while he is eating, slip the ropes over his neck and then the halter or headcollar over his nose. The headcollar is then buckled up, or the halter slipped over his ears. Never rush up to a pony, waving the halter or a bridle. A pony that is difficult to catch will improve if he is visited occasionally without being caught, and offered a tit-bit. He can also be turned out in a snugly-fitting headcollar so he is ready to be held.

**Why grooming?**
Grooming is cleaning and smartening up a pony so that he looks his best. It is also necessary to remove all mud and dirt from under the saddle and girth area so that he is comfortable and not rubbed. Outdoor ponies do not need the grease removed from the skin and coat, as this repels the cold and wet; they do need the mud and dead hair removed and the hair of the mane and tail separated and untangled.

# GROOMING IMPLEMENTS

**Dandy brush** - A brush with long, strong bristles for removing mud and loose hair.
**Body brush** - An oval brush with short, soft bristles for removing grease, dust and hair. Also for brushing manes and tails.
**Curry comb** - A metal tool for removing dirt and hair from the brush.
**Mane comb** - Metal, or equally strong, comb for tidying the mane and top of the hairs of the tail.
**Water brush** - A soft brush for wetting the mane and tail to flatten stray hairs. Also for washing hooves.
**Hoof pick** - A hooked metal tool for removing dirt and stones from the underside of the hoof.
**Sponge** - For cleaning the eyes, nose and dock (in that order).
**Stable rubber** - A soft cloth for polishing the coat after grooming.

**Tips**
Always brush in the direction the coat grows. Do not over-brush the mane and tail with the dandy-brush, or the hairs will break and fall out. Always inspect the feet for stones or other objects before riding.

**Manes and tails**
Never cut the mane with scissors. To shorten and thin, take a lesson from an expert on 'pulling', which means pulling out the long hairs. The tail may be cut, or 'banged' straight at the bottom so that it falls 3 inches below the hock. Mountain and Moorland ponies can be left untrimmed for protection against inclement weather and flies.

# SHOEING

**The farrier**
The farrier trims, shoes and attends to the pony's feet. He is a specialist in this area and understands diseases and remedial shoeing.

**The blacksmith**
The blacksmith shoes and trims the feet and generally has a good understanding of the problems in this area. Both blacksmith and farrier have to be qualified to practice. The blacksmith also works in iron products, both ornamental ironwork and machinery repairs. Many are capable wheelwrights.

**The hoof**
A pony's foot, or hoof, is not a solid lump of horn. Only the shell is of horn. Within are bones, nerves, ligaments, blood and tissue. Underneath the shell, on the base of the foot, is a triangular spongy pad termed the 'frog'. This is an anti-slip and anti-concussion pad.

**Growth**
The pony's outside horn of the foot is growing all the time. Therefore if it is not worn away on the hard surface it will need trimming, just like a person's fingernails. Ponies who work on roads and hard, stony surfaces will need shoeing to avoid over-wear and an uneven surface to the hoof. Horn growth requires trimming and attention every 6-8 weeks. If the shoes are not worn out they can be removed, the hoof trimmed and the shoe replaced. If the shoes are left on for longer, the horn will grow too long, the nails of the shoes (clenches) will work lose and rise, and the cramped foot will develop corns.

**Regular care**
We now know that a pony's foot must be checked every 6-8 weeks to ensure that the horn is the correct length and that if he is shod, the shoe is not worn through and still fits snugly. Ponies who do not wear shoes may well need the wearing surface of the foot smoothed even with the rasp, and any chips or cracks in the horn observed and dealt with.

pressure and alter foot shape and action.

**Competition shoes**
Competition horses are often shod with shoes incorporating holes in which non-skid studs can be fixed. Show ponies wear light shoes to encourage long, low action, while driving ponies are encouraged to raise their knees by shoeing with thick, heavy shoes.

**Remedial shoeing**
Some ponies need special shoeing to assist disease and pressure in the foot, and to correct foot and action faults. Specially designed shoes can relieve

**No worries**
Do not worry about the nails being driven through the hoof. The nails only go through the insensitive horn, running clear of the sensitive inner parts.

# PONY VETERINARY

## Worming
Every pony requires regular worming. Internal worms cause a pony to become thin, lethargic and an unhealthy appearance. Worm doses, given either by mouth in the form of a paste syringe, or as a powder in the feed, can be obtained from a veterinary surgeon with his advice on type and amount given. A worm dose should be given every three months.

## Teeth
A pony's molar teeth may become uneven or sharp, so that he cannot grind his food properly. Old ponies particularly suffer with this problem. Teeth should be inspected by the vet if the pony shows signs of dropping uneaten grains or hay from his food.

## Colic
Colic is 'tummy ache' in a pony. It can be caused by bad feeding, drinking too much water after a feed, worms and, among other causes, eating too many windfall apples. The pony will appear very uncomfortable, walking around in circles, rolling frequently, sweating and looking at his sides. Call the vet as soon as colic is suspected.

40 RIDING

### Lameness

The pony is lame when he moves with uneven strides, taking smaller steps with the lame leg and carrying more of his weight on the sound. First look in his hoof for stones or a nail puncture. Feel all down the suspected leg for cuts, bruises, heat or puffiness. If you are puzzled, or the pony has some obvious wound that requires treatment, call in the vet.

### Laminitis

This is a disease of the feet, mainly found in small, over-fat ponies. It is caused by too much rich grass, or too much hard feed. The pony's diet should be watched carefully in spring and summer when the grass is at its best. If the pony is reluctant to walk, sits back on its hind legs placing the front ones out stiffly, puts his weight pressure on the heel of the foot, and if the feet are very warm, suspect laminitis. The pony is in great pain which the vet can relieve. Call him immediately.

### Coughing and influenza

All ponies should be vaccinated against influenza and coughing. Indeed you cannot show a pony that does not carry a vaccination certificate. Register your pony with a vet and he will take care of the necessary procedure and booster vaccinations. Any signs of coughing or a runny nose and 'off colour' should be reported to him immediately.

### Sweet itch

This is an exasperating allergy to a certain midge which causes the pony to rub at his mane and tail, and often the hair over his wither and croup. There are several applications and lotions obtainable at feed and tack shops, to massage into the area. The vet may suggest an anti-allergy injection. Keep the pony away from flies, especially at dawn and dusk when the midges bite.

# THE PONY'S HOME

**Fields and paddocks**
The pony's health depends to a large extent on the way his field or paddock is looked after. If there are more weeds than grass, or if there are poisonous plants he may nibble, he will not remain healthy. Alternatively if a single pony has a large field of good grass, he may become over-fat, lazy, or contract laminitis.

**Poisonous weeds and trees**
Ragwort is the most common of the poisonous paddock plants. It is even more toxic when dead than when alive. Ragwort should be pulled up, collected and taken away and burned. Paddocks bordering on gardens should be carefully scrutinised for invading poisonous plants. Watch out for laburnham, foxglove, cherry bark, conifers and thorn apple. Other poisonous weeds include ransoms, meadow saffron, green bracken, buttercup, celendine, St. John's wort, hemlock, water dropwort, ground ivy and fool's parsley. The yew tree is well known as being poisonous to ponies. Look up all these plants, in good reference books and be able to recognise each of them.

### Weeds

Nettles, thistles and docks are among the worst non-poisonous paddock-invading weeds. These can be removed by chemical spraying or regular cutting. If the ground is sprayed, the pony must not be allowed near that ground for 3 weeks.

### Droppings

Most weeds appear where the pony's droppings accumulate. Most ponies have special 'latrine' areas, keeping their feeding grounds clean and fresh.

Picking up the droppings using a wheel barrow is hard work, but leaves a tidy, well cared for paddock. The pony is also less likely to re-infest himself with worms. Alternatively droppings can be spread by harrowing over the area. In this case, remember the regular worm doses.

### Fertilising

If the grass is very sparse and poor, it can be fertilised by scattering granules over the area or spraying with a liquid fertiliser. You will need help with this, and advice on type and quantity of fertiliser. An agricultural merchant or garden centre will advise. Again, the pony may have to be kept off the ground. For spraying chemicals or fertilising, the field can be split with an electric fence, treating each side separately, on still days so that chemicals cannot blow across and contaminate the grazing area.

**Warning:** Eating chemically sprayed grass can kill a pony. If possible remove him far from the ground, in a borrowed field, until it is safe to return him.

# A STABLE HOME

**Good housekeeping**
Ponies who live in stables should be 'mucked out' every day. A pony left to stand in deep, wet manure will suffer from soft, crumbly feet and even 'thrush', when the feet ooze a nasty smelling pus - a serious foot infection. Scoop the clean straw, shavings or other bedding to the side of the stable, barrow out the wet and dirty parts, and sweep the floor clean. If possible leave the bedding up for a while so that the floor may dry. The muck heap, preferably a short distance from the stable to avoid smells and flies, should be kept neat and tidy. Well rotted manure is useful for the garden.

**Haynets**
A haynet, stuffed with hay and hung in the stable or field shelter, saves the pony treading good hay into dirty bedding or mud and thus wasting it. Haynets should be hung as high as possible to prevent the pony pawing at it when empty and thus getting his foot caught up. Always tie a haynet with a safety quick release knot.

**Water**
Whether in a stable or field, there should always be a constant supply of fresh, clean water. Important: fill the water bucket before feeding if it is empty.

**Mangers**
A pony's manger is like your dinner plate. Keep it clean. No pony likes the remains of the last feed mixed in with the next. If he does not 'clear up', look into his diet and health. You may be over-feeding, he may be off-colour or his teeth may need seeing to.

## Rugs

Some ponies wear a weatherproof New Zealand rug when they are turned out during the day because the rider is unable to exercise them. When the stabled pony comes in, this is changed for a warm night rug.

Ponies that stay in after ridden exercise can wear a day rug. This is usually less warm and smarter than a night rug as the pony is unlikely to lie down and dirty it.

Often a stabled pony is clipped right out. This means that all his coat is removed and often the fetlocks and hair on the legs too. If he is ridden through wet, clinging mud, his skin will not be protected by the hair, and the mud drying on the skin may give him a condition known as mud fever. Wash and dry his legs thoroughly if he comes in plastered in mud, and rub Vaseline or cream into the skin.

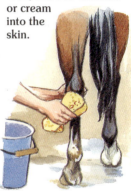

## Fresh air

Fresh air is important to the stabled pony. Few if any require the top door shuttering at night and then only in the very worst of weather. Draughts are a different matter and should be avoided.

# EQUESTRIAN CAREERS

**Pony mad**
If you are a real pony addict, you will want to spend all your time with horses and ponies once you have left school. It is never too soon to start thinking about, and preparing for a career with horses. There are plenty of things you can do - but you will need to be very good at your chosen career if you want to earn your living by it.

**Schoolwork**
Some equestrian careers require you to take 'A' levels, while others will certainly need 'GCSE' in English and Maths. If you want to work abroad, languages are important. So don't neglect your schoolwork - it may cost you your chosen career.

**Teaching**
Should you become a really good rider and pass all the Pony Club tests and British Horse Society exams, you may like to teach. There are a great many Equestrian Centres and Riding Schools who require good teachers. Some riders specialise and teach only jumping, dressage or some other activity. There are lots of opportunities.

**Racing**
Girls as well as boys now work in racing stables, and some become jockeys. For the more academic, racing stables require secretaries, accountants and stud clerks to keep their books in order.

### Showing

Showing stables require riders to break, school and work with their show stock. This could lead to your own showing 'yard'. It is even possible to make a living in show jumping, either working as a groom and travelling the world with a well known jumper, or, if you have enough money and good horses, show jumping yourself!

### Stud work

Working on a stud where horses and ponies are bred can be very interesting. You could be employed as a trainee as a start and work your way up. Alternatively many Agricultural Colleges offer courses on stud work.

### Veterinary

This really does mean hard work at school and 'A' levels in science subjects. A veterinary course takes several years and the work is challenging. If you prefer veterinary nursing, you can learn with a local vet.

### Holiday work

Trekking and holiday centres require people to take their riders out for the day. This is usually a seasonal job, but great fun.

### Information

If you are interested in a career with horses, write to the British Horse Society or the equivalent society or federation in another country, and ask for information, leaflets, brochures, etc. on your chosen career or any other role you may be interested in. Local council and career agencies will also help. Meanwhile, as you grow up, look around and see how other people earn their livings with horses and ponies.

# A PONY - A FRIEND

**Ponies, ponies, ponies**

Not everyone is fortunate to have a pony of their own to love and care for. Nevertheless you can still enjoy limitless fun by helping other people to look after theirs - and claim a ride in return! You may even find someone who wants their pony exercised once you are old enough and capable enough. Always treat every pony you come across with kindness and encouragement. Ponies respond to children they respect, so always be firm, but never, never lose your temper.

**Not a machine**

The better the pony is looked after and ridden, the more rewarding it becomes for the rider. A pony likes routine. In fact, he has a built-in clock and expects feeding and riding at certain times. It makes him feel secure. Boredom and its opposite, overwork are his worst enemies. Remember to visit him even if you do not want to ride. He will be pleased to see you - and your tidbit!